Grass is fo

"The goats want some grass,"
said uncle.

So we gave the goats some grass.

"The chickens want some rice," said uncle.

So we gave the chickens some rice.

Uncle said, "The horse wants some hay."

So we gave the horse some hay.

4

What do the children want?" uncle asked.
Some grass? Some rice? Some hay?"

No! No! No!" we shouted.

Uncle laughed and said, "Children are not goats. Children are not chickens. Children are not horses."

6